THE SPEED OF THE WHEEL IS UP TO THE POTTER

NEW CANADIAN POETS SERIES

This series of titles from Quarry Press charts new directions being taken in contemporary poetry by presenting the first book-length work of innovative writers.

Other titles in the series include *Undressing the Dark* by Barbara Carey, *The Big Life Painting* by Ron Charach, *Poets 88*, and *Stalin's Carnival* by Steven Heighton.

NC
PS

The Speed of the Wheel

Is Up to the Potter

SANDY SHREVE

Quarry Press

The publisher thanks the Ontario Arts Council and
The Canada Council for assistance in publishing this book.

CANADIAN CATALOGUING IN PUBLICATION DATA

Shreve, Sandy
The speed of the wheel is up to the potter

(New Canadian poets series)
ISBN 0-919627-79-X

I. Title. II. Series.

PS8587.H75S63 1990 C813'.54 C90-090165-9
PR9199.3.S47S63 1990

Cover art entitled "The Garden" by Veronica Desjardins.
Reproduced with permission of the artist.

Design and imaging by ECW Type & Art, Sydenham, Ontario.
Printed and bound in Canada by Hignell Printing, Winnipeg, Manitoba.

Distributed in Canada by University of Toronto Press,
5201 Dufferin Street, Downsview, Ontario M3H 5T8,
and in the United States of America by Bookslinger,
502 North Prior Avenue, St. Paul, Minnesota 55104.

Published by *Quarry Press, Inc.*, P.O. Box 1061, Kingston,
Ontario K7L 4Y5, and P.O. Box 348, Clayton, New York 13624.

in memory of Joan Wood

CONTENTS

Allegiances

ALLEGIANCES

"But och! I backward cast my e'e
on prospects drear!
An' forward though I canna see,
I guess an' fear!"
(Robert Burns, "To A Mouse")

I.

Rootbound

Indigenous forest, inched into the earth
a geological sinking of alder, birch, spruce,
the shrinking unnoticed, though stories
were told, when only the tips still showed,
of ancient giants displaced
by dwarves.

This marsh, a coffin of trampled paths.
Strewn between the thistle
and the lily
smudged footprints stumble
in wars as rooted
as petrified woodlands below

2.

Petroglyphs

The Micmac hand
a chisel of bone
petroglyphs etched
on cliffs of stone

Explorers name borders,
sandstone slates erode

3.

The Tantramar

Tintamarre
the Acadians named it —
a sound of many wings,
the rustle and call
myriads of birds create
in their autumn and spring

Translated
the word a racket —
cacophony of war,
of the settlers' forced migrations

4.

Settlers

arrive, brimming with
ancestral dreams of freedom,
of a piece of land, secure
from the snatch of avarice —
inhabit the vision
an ocean away from its origin.

Innocent the grip
of scattered fences —
unobtrusive, Acadians use
pockets of land the Micmac
continue to pass through

the conflict of property concepts
as yet harmless — there's
space to spare, share

❧

Uncertain words,
the stammer of translation
lapses, at first, to use
of the hands

hands of distant habit
unfamiliar hue, yet able to
manage an understanding.

Invisible the fist
in progress, gently introduced
with fingertips of friendship . . .

❧

5.

Minudie: 1755

In the silence after cease-fire
the tide disgorges corpses

Terror contagious, remains.
The memory of shrieks,
families clustered in doorways
then racing, stumbling,
chased to the waves — those
frantic strokes in the water
crippled with the speed of bullets.

Soldiers poke among bloated bodies —
already crows join the forage,
peck the startle from eyes
still wide with cries of surrender.

Oh soldier, did you notice
before your shot slashed the dawn
how the promise of morning
fingered the willow,
stretched to thaw the thin
sparkle of frost on the harvest

Sunlight latticed
through the first spring breeze
welds hands to the land's routines
which require the kind of
pause it takes,
back arched
from the spade or shuttle
to admire the spiral,
the precise glide and dive
of a marsh hawk's art of survival

that aspect of freedom in bonds
you need, to feel you belong

    (other bonds hover
    bonds of territorial conquest:
    the enthralling visions
    of crowned vultures

    whose spells sometimes
    are broken)

❖

What haunted them
were images of ice-sculpted
kings and religions,
the demands of various allegiances,
how a river claims two sides
though one appears much
as the other

8.

'Conquest'

The war-weary Micmac grasps
a hatchet, the blade
gouges the earth,
this burial
a ceremony of peace
not defeat.

Shallow roots protrude —
infestations of invaders' fences
bulge to barricades against
nomadic ways, invent
legal claims to land
the Natives never ceded

A foreign civilization
exuding words, assurances
that transcribe to treachery:

a hammer and a wedge
in a brittle wind

9.

Baskets

A memory embroiders her
in ankle-skirt and shawl —
a spot amidst the spittle
on the sidewalk.

Mending baskets gathering curb dust
her hands, if noticed
scoffed for the bother

   (her face long faded
   from a shuttered view)

Woven in between these strips of bark
an invisible herstory.
Beads entwined in intricate designs,
once an artful need in being, her work
tucked into these modern times,
a sideline 'cottage hobby.'

Starvation often just so many
unsold baskets distant,
the women,
fingers young or grown arthritic,
keep on weaving

10.

Icons

An unmapped Micmac burial ground
evergreen edges once safe
from the fray of distant towns, now
shredded through the center

Land claims debates continue/
a bulldozer spews an artifact
confused with stones in sludge.

Once whittled with the precision
of a hand warmed
to the spirit of the bone
this figure claimed a noble symmetry:

symbol of a sculptor's eternal guardian
the totem captures no-one's eye —
steel teeth of a modern machine
crush it with uncanny ease

II.

Fort Beauséjour: 1984

Children hide/seek in casemates
free at last from the museum's
artifacts of peace and war,
eyes still blurred
from history observed
through glass-cased displays

Sunday strollers on ramparts
idly clutch
a litany of pamphlet facts
thinned and sifted,
watch the Transcontinental
glinting in the distance,
admire miles of marsh
an occasional barn,
curse the onslaught
from the Cumberland shore —
perpetual wind
insisting strands of hair
onto camera lenses

Cannons stand sentinel
on a stolen hillside

DISTANCES

When I was a kid
we rarely travelled
the lengthy nine-mile stretch
from Sackville to Amherst

When we did, I'd begin the trip
devouring mixtures of marshland scents
blended by Fundy Bay winds.
Then bored, I'd fidget the miles away
devising schemes for the endless
cat-tails and reeds
dykes and grey-walled hay barns
barricaded at either end
by the main-street hubbub
of the Tantramar towns

In my twelve-year-old innocence
I'd suggest the fields were
idle and wasted:
we could solve the problems
of overpopulation and underhousing, if we
distended the towns to one city.

Now I drive a mere nine miles each day
from my Vancouver home to a Burnaby job.
The sterile scenery carries
no fragrance, except for the fumes
from other cars of other commuters
or a poignant blast
from a pulp mill imposed
some miles up the coast

The single mark
to distinguish the cities
is a battered sign, crammed
between houses and stores and industry
that clutter the roadside

SOUND

of the city, this evening
a deep drone thrumming across
the water to mountains
rebounds back
to our residential porch,
rush-hour a long drawn
out memory, like endless
freight trains — boxcars
shoving themselves along nights
of a sleepless childhood,
resolving shadows to a merry-
go-round on quiet walls,
their sound, remote

yet close
enough to muffle crickets, as
now the chirping of birds
is a meek piercing of noise.

All this is abstraction —
sound of invisible source
as if inevitable, constant,
something that cannot be stilled

though we know it comes
from machines dependent
on women and men, we think of
this hum as the heart of the City,
forget there are people with hands
at the controls

NIGHT LIGHTS ON THE GEODESIC DOME

for Kate Braid

You mentioned the welder you imagined
working late into the night, how
the sparks you saw flying from a torch
held by hands still fondly binding triangles
kept you fascinated
until you realized the delicate
firefly dance
was only an erratic flashing of bulbs.

Construction of this sphere never
intrigued me. It has always
looked cold, the metal more
like tinsel ribbed with acrylic
inexplicably curved to a finished glitter,
an irritating scrape
across my eyes

This lattice of arched angles
seemed like sterile growth around a void —
but last night, driving by

I think I saw your welder
dancing on the dome

COMMUTERS

The whole way home, I was stuck
under the wet, black half
of a sun-shower sky,
and this, only the fifth
of forty-five Mondays
to survive this year

Half an hour later, when I
yanked up the brake at my door
all I recalled
was the wipers lashing at
sun-sparkled raindrops

So now, I'm curious — just how many
other commuters were jolted
from their mobile dreams
to panic at my blind cruising.

I've watched them, other days
of the week, perched
behind the windshields
of their private fantasies,
all assuming their identities
are as camouflaged
as the beaked and feathered ad man
playing the fool for Kentucky Fried
on the side of a highway:
this one giving the boss or whoever
regular hell, fists gripping
a handy steering wheel,
that one just kind of
smirking into space, or another
reliving a distant kiss . . .

All these charades playing games
on their faces.
Some, already dissolving, tossed
aside with the seatbelt;
others, stiffening into creases
between lips and eyes, forced
into kitchens and living rooms —
a grinding silence here, too many drinks
turned to fury there,
a wish for a different lover
someone's desperate prayer.

House-key in hand, I wonder
which of those faces was mine
as I drove, mesmerized
by my own torrent of mimes

HOME

At a certain time
of dawn
the cloud-covered alley
wears a dust-grey coat
and you move
through the folds
collecting refundable
meal tickets
from garbage cans

As daylight smooths
those shadows
our doors open
and you spend hours
pouring over
Chicago phone books.

Between jobs
we clerks sometimes talk
of unpleasant odours
and creases through
your suit and eyes —
soothing our fears
with rumours
of your past careers
and how you came
to call the Library
home

REGIONALISM

for Leona Gom

Suckled on the sugar-maple
sap of New Brunswick
I am inclined to a certain
narrow perspective:

Easterners turned B.C.ers
face my wrath
when they dare defend any
but Maritime syrup

And how I delight
in the plight of Prairie people
whose knowledge of maples comes
mainly from colouring books —
ah, they are so ripe
for training
in the finer tastes of life

NOSTALGIA

The austere Northumberland
shore's grey guard
withdraws behind
patches of herons
heaving their weight
to flight in panic, leaving
their nests to the hawk

As cottagers awake
to shrill spirals, I watch
old friends yearn
for the scattered birds'
pain to halt — but feel more
akin to the intruder

here for the first time in years,
circling their lives to seize
my idealized memories

LOST IN THIS CITY

After fifteen years, I still
get lost in this city.
Today I'm looking for traffic court,
able to pay the fine, though outraged,
tense with this and the uncertainty
of where in skid road I'm to go.

Pocketed, my fingers tighten
with what I know about these streets.
Ahead of me, a tall thin man
leaps from his amble in the crosswalk,
becomes a jack-in-the-box
attacking traffic,
his body a flailing X of anger

Further on, he's calm — aims
his arms along air,
squints behind his invisible sight

his eyes cold metal as he lowers
his hands, turns
to me, clenched in my coat, passing

JAYWALKERS

come at you in all shapes and sizes
all styles and shades of dress
and from every possible angle —
stab the leaded air with their eyes,
tangle the traffic with imagined chasms
their zigzag strides slash
in the pavement

These impatient pedestrians
(car keys jangling
                        in flapping pockets)
are hell on disc brakes and
tire treads, as they challenge nerves
to uninvited duels

The streets record such incidents
in blurred quilts of skid curves,
the black on grey, uninspired
works of modern art.
But surrounding the superficial scars
you can glimpse a grand design:
wisps of the jaywalkers' trajectories
criss-cross from curb to curb
in a mosaic, tinged
and shimmering
with the laughter that belongs
to small victories

MAGPIES IN THE PALM TREES

It is a long approach. The jet
sinks through a jaundiced gauze,
each porthole a pair of eyes
that cannot quite grasp the expanse
of this city, or imagine an opening
between clenched fists of buildings
where a plane might land.

On the ground, it is a harsh air.
Hardly breathable, it crawls
behind eyes, is an ache
as constant as crowds that shove
among palms pinned on boulevards
of perpetual buses and trucks and cars

And the wind. The wind can carry
a rain that falls like tar, or when it's
dust in the dry sun, will slap
at your white and naked eyes,
etch into them: the man
who sucks flames and spews them out
beside a frenzied intersection,
the child who peddles chiclets
to drivers at the light, the veiled
wailer crouched on a curb
behind the church — her hand
open like a wound

These scenes irritate, at first
draw tears. We listen
over tea in the evening
to explanations: politics, economics,
corruption — the chiaroscuro
to images locked in our heads
like negatives curled in cameras.

As days pass, we learn to avert
our eyes. Between museums and markets
admire blooming bougainvillaea cringing
against walls. And after Diego Rivera's
murals of revolution, emerge
into these streets of failed dreams
to scan stained leaves for screeching
magpies in the palm trees

Mexico City, 1986

VACATION

This is the year's
shortest season —
a brief reprieve
begged for at
a bargaining table
and arbitrarily allocated
as though the amount
of rest
required to forget
someone else's details
can be measured
according to the loyalty
shown to a company
by the number of years
spent in stagnation

❧

As we drive to the pace
of sunshine strobe-
lighting the windshield
through trees
we plot our escape
from excessive technologies
in which each of us
daily partakes:
search
for out of the way spots
where we can pitch our tent

and hug what survives
our destruction

ESCAPE

". . . in the zoo the view is always wrong."
                                 (John Berger, *About Looking*)

Receding behind the miles
our city hunches into itself,
a confined distance — like the look
on passengers' faces, asphyxiated
as a trapped seal's gaze
at the frightening delight of children
before it lumbers from platform
to pool, desperate for an ocean gateway.

❧

Eagles are everywhere on this island —
feathers smooth as the whites of our eyes
we spend hours on a cliff, watching them,
exotic in their paradise
of uncaged air

A fibre of sound tugs at our glance
as a harbour seal glistens past
oblivious to us listening
to the even gasp of its breathing
drawn in the open space between waves

Ecstatic as children
we stand between the swimmer
and the soaring —
longing for a closer look

HOMAGE

for Bill

This October the days languish
beneath layers of ashen air —
you can see this thicken at a distance,
point to the haze shrouding mountains
but only know you walk within it
by the weight of your lungs.

As you approach the park at dawn
a fragment of motion captures
your eye:
a solitary figure in black
shapes geometries of tai chi
with her limbs —
each angular arrival, sudden

yet smooth as new amber sliding
across the pallid sky:
a hushed moment of colour ·
fragile as dried flowers
streaks through the pollution

as she sculpts a small prayer
into sunrise
and you bow

Crumpled Smiles

THAT MAGIC TOUCH

I've been learning the ways
of word-processing — how to
manage the keys (quickly)
in an entranced dance
of the hands: which ones to touch
for first drafts, which for changes
keeping the printer busy while
I work (today, typists' efforts appear
on a screen, and a separate
tiny machine
puts them to paper for us, with an
impassive clatter)

On a break, I listen
for that magic music a skilled
typist creates, while Donna
next door, works away. At first
her printer prevails,
confounds me with a monotony
of sound. But then
it's silenced
and what remains
is the perfection of her fingers
caressing the keyboard —
the melody and rhythm
of pauses, complementing phrases

allegretto, andante, spiritoso

WHITE-OUT

Frenzied fingers type
faster faster
race the onslaught
of numbing numbers
to get the damned tables done.

But the eyes no longer co-operate.
figures wriggle and blur
in a dance these pupils
never learned

the brain balks, savours four
o'clock — then veers toward fears
of permanent dyslexia
from fluorescent-lit
statistics

Then he trots into the office
bent arm bulging
proofread pages, ticked
with changes
serves my cluttered desk
this extra dish.
Comments how, although
perhaps a bore, HE sometimes
wouldn't mind my job:
just sit all day and copy
someone else's work!

Furious
the fingers grip
liquid paper
bloated brush
poised

VDTs

It could almost be
a sci-fi film
the way the words
come up green, against
a black screen
flickering stress
and migraines,
prematurely
aging our eyes
with cataracts

But the future
remains
here
and as we listen
to vehement denials
of radiation dangers

we sit before
these machines
nurturing wounds —
nascent Luddites
not yet sure
of our grip

MENTAL CRUELTY

Books, piled high like a fortress
shelter each side of my desk
from all but her orders.
How many methods can exist
to mend spines and clean covers
I wonder
as she lurks behind my
backless stool and lectures,
as I stare at the workroom's
windowless wall, jaw clenched
in impatient silence.

Hers, the first-strike artillery
set for attack at will:
demeaning instructions, daily
dispensed, as regularly as time-
release capsules.
My stature shrinks twenty years
when my bosses, two feet away
discuss what tasks
I'll have time to do, without
asking me

Yet to complain
seems akin to an unwilling
warrior gone AWOL because
rain made muck of the trenches.
And anyway, mental cruelty
is only grounds for divorce
not concrete cause to launch
a grievance.

We'll need more
than a good union contract
to settle this dispute

THE BOOK TRUCK

"I won't support
across-the-board:
librarians deserve
much more than clerks."

And me there squatting
at her feet
on my knees
digging out dingy
volume after volume
from the book truck
stacking them in shelves
so I can clothe them later
with shining covers
bored and sneezing
from the dust
of the dreary back room

"Too bad if you can't
eat well on what you earn."

And my stomach growls
just as hard as hers
for lunch
while I wash books
sort books
stack books
shelve books,
while she sits, pensive
at her desk
reading journals I deliver,
answers questions
patrons ask

I still recall the day
I gave a woman
Atwood's novel
from the shelf where
I was filing books
and she bustled over
yelling: "Never
do that again —
send the borrower to me!"

Even if the book
is in my hand,
she's the librarian
not me:
I shelve books

GRIEVANCE PROCEDURE

I am listening to
a woman worried —
the harassment's there
though often so subtle
it evades articulation.

Not that she wants to grieve
this incident, or that
in union terms

(the concept of defiance
such a threat)

And yet she grieves —
trying hard not to cry, she
apologizes as I
offer tissues:

feeble things, only good
for absorption.

The office trashcan, congested
with such as these,
an archive of pain
collected and dumped
each day

WINGS

"Loyalty [to the employer] and some restrictions on the exercise of the right of free speech are required by the jurisprudence . . . whatever the private opinions of the workers may be."

(R. Bird, 1985 arbitration decision, SFU vs. AUCE Local 2)

The still grey of concrete walls
surrounds me
as I read, muttering
forbidden criticisms

interrupted by the scratch
of my hand turning pages
and an off-beat tinkering
at the ceiling.

A moth, parchment-like wings thin
as hissed syllables
butts at glass shackles,
encased light confused for the moon.

I could give these pages wings —
make of them children's
paper planes,
heed them, like the moth
spinning in deluded flight . . .

Overhead, the moth
wears desiccating wings,
continues its stunted search
dying against an artifice
of human sight

RESOLUTIONS

seems I feel like this every
night, lately. Not just tired,
skin worn clear through to the bone —
but ashamed. Yes, I guess that's it:
afraid someone I 'dealt with' today
might recognize me, on the street somewhere
one weekend, and whisper — sliding
the words behind an open hand, the way
you do when you do and don't
want the culprit to hear — "bitch, oh
she's really awful!"

by four each day I'm explaining away
all my abrupt actions, snide
remarks, with facts
of overworked and underpaid (how
can I keep the plastered smile
and calm from dissolving
to a decayed scowl, when everyone
claims my time simultaneously
for whatever's critical to them just then)
comes from government cutbacks, yes,
and layoffs; tech change — the illusion
that computers will do it all for us . . .

but as I was saying, every
night, lately — I come home reduced
to a thin howl, resolving
over and over again, not
to be impatient, sharp, short
with anyone — tomorrow
I'll take it all in stride
smiling: I'm a public service worker
here to ease your worries and fears

then tomorrow comes along:
Please, please, one thing at a time!
I hate to make you wait, but I'm just . . .

and I go home, breathing the foul odour
of yesterday, regurgitated,
resolving: Tomorrow . . .

LAUGHTER

Easy to envy that laughter
as it billows along the hallway,
drifts into every office
curling curtains like a summer breeze

    whoever has the chance
    will pop out to join her,
    chuckle in hand, anxious
    to make it last

    the rest of us bend back
    to our papers
    wearing borrowed smiles

You imagine she's happiness itself
until one day, mechanically
packaging each phrase in a laugh
she tells you her story
curling her fingers
in and out of fists

you search her face
find only crumpled smiles,
her laughter convulsing down the corridor
a windstorm pounding doors

OUR GIRL FRIDAY

Last week, every pencil I needed
sharpened at the feel of my reach,
paper clips untangled at my glance,
stacks of paper collated without one
licked finger;
a mere pat of my palm trained the stapler
to chatter perfect trilateral welds
into documents that distributed themselves
at the behest of my breath;
my fingers found required files
at the first touch,
labels emblazoned precise categories
onto folders in response to my very thoughts;
I had exact answers to everything
before I was asked

Last week efficiency was embodied in me.

But the people I work with
took all this for granted
and my paycheque remained the same

So this week I rewarded myself:
I exorcized the office
of its favourite possessive pronoun
and announced My Name,
I vaporized the word girl
and pronounced *WOMAN*,
then I slipped my fingers into scissors
released Friday
and walked off with her

LAID OFF

For years the job has been
within the reach of rolling over
to the early morning news, as close
to her hand as a habit.

One day the second-hand
ticks past six in silence
the old routine, an apparition
hovering in the emptiness

between frantic eyes and yesterday's
fantasy of sleeping in

SLOGANS

These few letters, extracted
from an alphabet that can formulate
anything, seem so
strong, each felt-penned word
a healer of wounds.

As if these phrases
will convince everyone else
to listen
we string them around our necks,
cardboard boundaries to
how we advertise ourselves on issues
seem feeble

But after mere hours, what we
could not fit into print
pricks our hearts with the silence
of pins —
there are so few passersby with time
for the text behind these messages.

We pace with the ink facing
strangers, hope they'll remember
at least one rectangle
of our semaphore,
each urgent word
bleeding into itself
like a bruise

STILL BLIND

It is something larger than you
or I, that determines how our words
will prickle the air between us

You with your urgent needs, and I
with mine, our hands
snatch at an invisible
twin-edged knife,
pierce each other's skin.

Each of us acts in the same
unspeakable play,
steeped in the thin curl
of predictable wounds
to the point where we fail
to recognize
the voices in each other's eyes

The chance to say, "Sorry"
say, "Let's try this again"
stomps off with the shudder
of our rudeness
scraping even at our backs.

We become one another's
evening complaint
over distant dinners,
strangers still blind
to the weapon in our grip,
still wielding the blade

we slash strips
of our lives away

ROUGH EDGES

Coming home, I am a razor
sawing through the purple hue
and scent of a spring evening,
rough edges slashing silk
to permanent ruin.

Each sip of wine nestles me
gently into muffled cloud, yet I
want to hurl this drink at the wall

in an instant of no particular decision
the air is thick with crystal slivers,
white paint, a sudden burgundy mural
of dribbling fingers.

I try to erase this witness
to my weakness. Nothing works.
I invite no-one over
afraid of questions —
what caused those faded marks
now pink rivers spilling out
from posters too small
to conceal articulate stains . . .

(what could I say,
lifting my favourite red
to lips in idle conversation)

So I spend nights alone
toasting failures,
eyeing the clean canvas
of another wall

CONSUMER COMPLAINT

It starts with the cat's white
whisker, stitched invisibly
into the rug — no
machine can inhale that,
you have to bend, snatch it
from the carpet's grasp

It's when you're half way un-
bent, you remember that
miserable man, his installment
plan for sanitized living — not
pouring sand on your carpet and
leaving you with the mess — oh, no
worse. Unravelling his all-frills
suction cup from the box,
plugging it in, then
dramatic
steps back

and runs that power head
all over your floor, even
attaches some gadget to dig out
the grunge between couch cushions

then forces you to look
at all your dirt

and just to clinch the sale
sees that whisker — says I bet
your machine can't pick that up
glides his over the spot
and it's gone

Damn machine's never
pulled that off since

WHITE LIES

Surely the child's eyes
betrayed the lie — despite
the calm assurance of words
delivered precisely the way
my father had earlier
formed them for me
(just in case we're not home,
this is what to say . . .)

But no. The census taker
hastily noted:
father, working — specific location;
number of children — sex, age;
mother, housewife — does not work.

Then left behind
her friendly smile,
subtle traces of cologne
and a child concealing
the fact of her mother's
typing at home for money,
a fact my parents feared
once ingested by any
government agency
would be smuggled through promises
of confidentiality
to income-tax inspectors
who should not know
of money coming in
unless it's going to be reported
and paid for.

This was my first lesson
in the higher education
of permitted 'little white lies' —
from which I learned
one truth about governments,
one falsehood about housewives

THE POTTER'S WHEEL

Type, collate, staple:
mass-producing memos
the way metal molds
race to create consumer cups
by the hundreds.

Later, my night-class
instructor says, the best way
to burst air-bubbles
is to precede kneading
with therapeutic pounding:
so I slam my slab of clay
against the work-bench
as if it was my typewriter
crashing through
the office window,
as though the clouds of dust
were cold keys
and black ribbons
billowing into oblivion

Then, smeared with the mucky
mass of centered clay, my hands
begin to mold the mug
nurse it, like a suckling child;
feet kick and brake the wheel
as rigid fingers shape the sides,
style grooves and ease
the form
from mind's eye
to kiln-readied green-ware:

as the wheel spins
so grows the clay —
and the speed of the wheel
is up to the potter

QUILTING BEE

So this is it, the female
job ghetto. Seems
to be a lot of us here

our cheeks crinkling into
weathered grins, fingers
pecking at paper, eyes
at the air

Days and nights
fragmented
as if
we were collecting shreds
of time
for a fabulous quilt.

Well, perhaps we are

Might just one day
sew it up into something

they claim can't be made

Vanishing Point

HUNTING SEASON

Home from the hunt
my father would alert my mother
to the size of his catch
with corresponding honks
of the horn

Inside the house
we would tense
to wheels grinding gravel,
set to count
the booty — or scrounge
leftovers for dinner.

As for the birds
each blare pronounced
their last dying cry,
silence was the sound
of their freedom

CHAMPIONS

I don't know where the dragons
came from — dotted designs
macabre colour schemes — reds purples
greens, taking shape the moment
I shut my eyes until I screamed

Always, it was my mother
rushing in with comfort,
fabricating tales for me
as her steady hand stroked
my shoulder, cheek
explaining away alien imaginings
so I could learn to capture
demons in the act of transformation
from wrinkles on the pillow slip . . .

Entranced with her fables, I
never sensed a tremor
in those strong hands, stroking
my hair as she held me
talking   talking
at the window
of groggy giants, stumbling
from sleep to the lanes
about to roll another game:
each thunder clap a gutter ball,
a spare, a strike —
the score tolled in crescendoing decibels
sheeting a charcoal sky in terse
eclipses of white,
my cringing calmed with her assurance
that these were simply wild salutes
to every passing champion.

My mother webbing stories
for her children, ceaseless
as the patterns of rain,
watching it all with us so we'd
be fascinated, unafraid

the creases of her terror, veiled
though she ached for a hand
on her cheek

TAKING BACK THE NIGHT

A woman, alone at a window
shudders as she watches
the dark outside

House after house it's the same.
Separately framed, hands
clench sills.

The hour has reverted
to an early dark —
each of us, last Sunday morning
got up, obedient, fingered
our own clocks back
to standard time

no time now for that
after dinner stroll
when we could breathe in the hush
of early evening air. Already
it's night, and so far
only our slogan
has retrieved it from fear

So far, instead of walking
we rage inside
and stare

ABORTION

Prepped
jabbed
anæsthetized —
the saline chill
prickles its way
through my veins

My womb
one more piece
in the hospital's
monotonous
assembly line,
soon scraped clean
of the thrill
to feel
I am pregnant!
Of the fears —
how could I
raise a child
alone and poorly paid,
scraped with the same
bored precision
as are fish
when gutted
for freezing.

Discharged,
clutching the cold
religious pamphlets
birth control handbooks
and accusing eyes,
I march
with pro-choice parades
knowing even they
can't make necessity
easy

HEIRLOOMS

The cut is perfect —
ivory figures
chiselled to the eye
of a stranger's
image of chessmen.

The artist
perhaps long dead
was never known to me,
the work
is an heirloom now
handed down from my father,
some thing he cherished
which therefore speaks
of him

In my turn
I'll pass along this set
or someone who loves me
will claim it for a memory
of who I was

What then, becomes
of my father —
and who was
the artist

VISITING RITES

The caretaker led me here, his
aging legs more
able directions than words.
Our breaths thread a maze
of pathways — so many grey barricades,
alone I would have peered
at the surface of so many deaths
to find yours.

I have no garland of blossoms
for your headstone
as if their slow wilting
would be insults,
yet my fingers close around a cold
emptiness
and I kneel, awkward
with twenty years of absence

What is there to say to a grave?
I am your grown daughter, too practical
for this futile search
over bones

small clouds of my silence
settle on colourless stubble
as I bead feeble memories
translucent and ephemeral
as dew

PUBLIC EXECUTION

"Didn't your society use rituals . . . like your . . . public executionings —"
"We didn't do that! That was the old times, way before."
                              (Marge Piercy, *Woman on the Edge of Time*)

The tug of an abandoned ritual
draws our hands to colosseums
we keep fine-tuned in our living rooms.

Whatever's on will do — though usually
we flip the dial to something action-packed,
adjust to the contrast of mundane days.

Of course, like all our friends
we reject the worst — accept
into the secret recesses of our minds
only shows that we can rationalize:
    a good plot, no gore (well, minimal —
    you can't, after all, have mystery
    without murder — or if one week it's
    extreme then it's meaningful, or an
    aberration for that program);
    the detectives are sort-of feminist;
    the cop's rough, but really cares . . .

Snuggled inside these fictions
of heroes and villains, today
in Nicaragua or Guatemala
at Nanoose Bay or Main
and Hastings
can be ignored:

here we root for good defined
for us, within the confines
of one elusive hour at a time.
But now: you've caught us, willing
pre-determined plots. Witnessed
our applause — all those
bored subconscious thumbs
twitching

CANADIANS DRIVING THE I-5 WHILE THE U.S. BOMBED LIBYA

Maybe five miles from where
we drove, a sheen in sagging clouds
throbbed an orange pain,
a ragged reflection of
what must have been
a street, or even a whole town
in flames, the crash and scream
of disaster, silenced to us
by our distance

Exchanging possible causes
we veered away from tragedy —
forgot, after awhile, about
strangers cringing from a morning
of searing dust and rubble.

The spin of tires through
futile rain on the pavement
made a sizzling sound,
their mantra
hissing us along
a turnpike of complacency

NO LIFE

Darkness stalks him
through thick silence
until its pursuit
meets a sleep that tunnels
to exploding vistas
where he sheds
strangers' blood
in desperate exchange
for his own life —
the noble cause
of politics and leaders
blurred beneath death

Days, he chisels memories
to find the time
when he believed
the governments' wars
could end war
and fighting was a job
as clean as it looks
on the TV screen
where the armed forces'
ads burst
with tanks and training
in harmless target
practice —
brazenly proclaiming
"There's No Life Like It!"

REMEMBRANCE DAY

Words of humbled glory
surround these services
with the inner emptiness of wreaths

military parades march a peace
sharp as holly, pricking
a schizophrenic dream
that bleeds red as poppies
in the opiate of their seeds

VANISHING POINT

Missing children have faces
on moving vans,
there is a number to dial

Political prisoners appear in papers
adopted,
there are letters to write

Actions we can grip
with our fingers
require re/cognition

♧

In self-hypnosis comfort
is all-important.
You have to stay in this position
for the duration —
imagine yourself at ease like this
for hours
content with inactivity

Guide your mind through each muscle, limb,
pack every pain
in a box just large enough

watch it penetrate cranial bone
disappear
into air,
a distant pinprick

♧

We are capable of convincing ourselves
anything is true:

mesmerized, anguish vanishes —
we can raise a whole arm
without moving a muscle

SUPERSTITION

I have an amber cameo
set in time-tarnished bronze.
If you were to inspect
her face and mine
you'd see that both
are cracked and patched —
products of two accidents
we each survived by chance

   (the first, I salvaged and repaired her
   the second, she was simply there)

To think my safety might be linked
to a common piece of jewellery
is, of course, quite ludicrous

Still, I always wear the necklace

CLOUDS

MUSHROOM: *1. A fleshy, rapidly growing, umbrella-shaped fungus . . . ; especially, the common, edible field mushroom . . . and certain poisonous varieties loosely called toadstools.*
(Funk and Wagnalls Standard College Dictionary)

How can I describe clouds
to make you see them:

as stippled, streaked, or feathered?
billowing pillows of white?
foreboding, frowning, glowering?
scarlet, vermilion, crimson
or grey?

all echo cliches
though the clouds defy us — keep
coming back to challenge language

until, so used to their presence
we flatten them with
scientific names —
cumulus, cirrus, stratus, nimbus . . .

or transform them to euphemism
in the common form
of a mushroom — render
what creates this shape
easy to swallow

the warning, a tasteless phrase
on our tongues

ACKNOWLEDGEMENTS

Some of these poems have appeared in *Auce Provincial News, Canadian Dimension, event, Fireweed, The Fisherman, Hysteria, Out of Line, Poetry Canada Review, Pottersfield Portfolio, The Public Employee, Quarry, Raven, Waves, West Coast Review, Writing*; and in the anthologies *East of Main, Going for Coffee, Celebrating Canadian Women, Coffee Break Secrets* (U.S.A.), *Piece by Piece You Deliver Yourself*, and *Women and Words: The Anthology*. The poem "No Life" was part of the Women and Words Peace-Write Campaign (1985-1986), "Slogans" was distributed as a broadsheet during the Vancouver Mayworks Festival, 1988, and "Sound" is on a broadsheet published by the Vancouver Industrial Writers Union (1990). Some of the poems have also been broadcast on Vancouver Co-operative Radio and CBC *Anthology*.

With thanks to numerous friends for their support, criticism, and encouragement; special thanks to Bill Twaites and Bronwen Wallace.